D1433056

RV Buyer's Handbook

WALT GERBER

ARCHWAY
PUBLISHING

This book is a work of non-fiction. Unless otherwise noted, the author
and the publisher make no explicit guarantees as to the accuracy of
the information contained in this book and in some cases, names of
people and places have been altered to protect their privacy.

Archway Publishing books may be ordered through booksellers or by contacting:

Archway Publishing
1663 Liberty Drive
Bloomington, IN 47403
www.archwaypublishing.com
1 (888) 242-5904

ISBN: 978-1-4808-8291-1 (sc)
ISBN: 978-1-4808-8292-8 (e)

Library of Congress Control Number: 2019915829

Print information available on the last page.

Archway Publishing rev. date: 11/08/2019

Contents

About the Author

Having camped regularly since his childhood, the author is close to the RV community. Over the years, he has owned eight different RVs and is currently living in a 42-foot fifth wheel full time. While working as a Level 2 NRVIA Certified RV Inspector through the National Recreational Vehicle Inspectors Association (www.nrvia.org), he has encountered many used RVs that had significant hidden problems which would ultimately put them in the category of "money pits" for the buyer. Similarly, a few new units were ultimately considered "lemons", ending up in litigation.

Many first-time buyers simply have no idea what they are getting into. Guided by this knowledge, the author was driven to prepare this Handbook. It will ease the process of selection, which will greatly improve everyone's RV experience.

Acknowledgement

I want to thank my friend Gail Taylor, for spending countless hours editing, asking questions and rearranging the subject matter so it all made sense. Without her tenacity and dedication, this handbook would not have been possible.

Introduction

Purchasing an RV is one of life's "big purchase" decisions. What is needed is a guide to selecting the RV features that best fit the potential camping style of the buyer. As more and more first-time buyers enter the market, the internet has become the place to go for information. For example, there are numerous detailed and comprehensive articles about RV refrigerators; however, an RV buyer doesn't need to know how an RV refrigerator operates in order to choose the right size unit to keep the food cold. By *unit* do I mean the RV or the fridge? The answer is generally "the larger the refrigerator, the larger the RV."

This book is written to provide a single source of help to guide you through the process of choosing, equipping and enjoying your RV purchase. The guidance herein attempts to cover most RVs but it is not possible to cover all types ever manufactured. Always keep this Handbook in your RV to use as reference in understanding how the systems work properly, and what to do when they don't.

1

Which RV Is Right For You?

Recreational Vehicles should not be confused with tiny homes. Those are generally constructed to be parked in a permanent or semi-permanent location, whereas RVs are designed to readily move about. The comparisons between the two are beyond the scope of this book.

Choosing an RV is as personal as choosing a pair of shoes. Think of fit and function.

The size generally relates to how many it will sleep. An RV advertised to sleep six can be misleading. The bedroom area usually has a queen bed, the couch folds out to sleep two, and the kitchen table converts into a small sleeping area for two. With this layout, you literally reconfigure the living area for sleeping and put it back again for daytime use. A bunk bed floor plan is an option for families with children. It reduces the need to daily convert sleeping/living areas, hence keeping the RV reasonably small. The point is to understand what is required to accommodate everyone. More permanent sleeping arrangements equate to a larger and heavier RV, a higher price and a larger tow vehicle.

For additional floor space, consider a floorplan that incorporates one or more slide-out rooms. The slide-out consists of three walls, floor, ceiling and windows. It is incorporated as part of the main structure of the RV. An electromechanical or hydraulic mechanism allows the slide-out to be pulled into the main frame of the RV when traveling, to keep the overall width of the RV to a legal limit of eight feet. Slide-out rooms increase the overall living area and are now offered even in smaller RVs.

A Motor Home advantage while on the road, over a Towable, is that you can make lunch or use the restroom without going outside. You cannot ride in a towable unless it is a Fifth Wheel but some states prohibit riding in a towable of *any* type. Check with the State Motor Vehicle Department everywhere you will travel to ensure compliance with local laws.

If you are considering purchasing a towable, the vehicle you presently own will affect your buying decision unless you are able to replace it. Having the right-sized tow vehicle is **critical** to the safety of everyone on the road. Look closely at the RVs on the highway; you will see many undersized tow vehicles riding nose high while the trailer is nose down. Watch them sway when a tractor trailer goes by. That same type of undersized tow vehicle can also be seen in the slow lane going uphill using a lower gear with the engine screaming. Then, when that combo heads downhill the brakes are smoking and the engine is still over-revving. This situation is an accident looking for a place to happen!

Matching Vehicle to Trailer

The information in this section is a guide to help buyers avoid dangers of driving an improperly matched tow vehicle and trailer. I personally observed an RV sales person—I'll keep the dealer anonymous—tell a potential buyer looking at an RV with three slide-outs, that it could be towed safely with a half-ton truck rated to tow 5,000 pounds. The trailer dry weight was 8,300 pounds. Do you see the problem here? Before you make your final buying decision on either tow vehicle or trailer, seek professional advice from a reputable RV dealer or vehicle manufacturer.

Get the right tow vehicle for the job. The internet is full of videos of towing mishaps, many of which are caused simply by too much trailer and not enough tow vehicle. Give yourself at least 1,000 pounds of extra tow capacity. I call it "towing headroom".

For example, I have used two different trucks to pull two different trailers, each with 1,000 pounds of towing headroom. Frequently I traveled on the same 500 mile route that included some hills but nothing mountainous. I was able to easily keep up with traffic on the flat parts, but on the hills each truck did a lot of shifting. This is why I set the *minimum* towing headroom to 1,000 pounds.

There is an abundance of information on the internet about gasoline vs diesel for all RVs. Each engine has its application and the appropriate decision should take into consideration weight, fuel economy and maintenance costs. Research will show that, for the bigger rigs, the right diesel powertrain will enable you to keep up with the flow of traffic on any terrain.

How Much Trailer Can My Vehicle *Safely* Pull?

For your safety, know the numbers. The data plate is usually located inside the driver's side door frame in the latch assembly area listing the appropriate information.

Look for the gross combination weight rating, or GCWR.

This is the total *combined* weight of tow vehicle *and* any potential trailer's weight as set by the manufacturer for safety.

Do not confuse with the gross vehicle weight rating, or GVWR. This is *only* the weight of the vehicle including fuel, hitch, added accessories, pets, passengers and personal belongings (no trailer).

Add your GVW "gross vehicle weight" plus the total weight of the trailer *loaded* with everything aboard.

So, when dealing with the trailer weight, to calculate the GVWR, **loaded** is the key word. The RV manufacturer lists the dry weight on a tag, usually on front driver's side. This is the trailer weight as built at the factory with all tanks empty. To that you must add your *stuff*—food, clothing, added equipment, including everything in all storage areas. And you must assume the water tanks are full. Water weighs 8.4 pounds per gallon and should be factored in the calculation. You may start out with mostly empty tanks, but as you go from day to day you will have added water weight until you dump the tanks. Additionally, assume your propane tanks are full and add that weight to the total. For the per-tank propane calculation use the following values:

> ➢ 20-pound full propane tank = 38 pounds
> ➢ 30-pound full propane tank = 55 pounds
> ➢ 40-pound full propane tank = 71 pounds

Weight estimates are just that—estimates. When in doubt, estimate high. As I have mentioned, always ensure you have more than ample towing headroom because you are almost always going to want to add items to your RV as you travel. Your storage areas will fill up fast with things like a portable grill, folding table and chairs, tools, an extra cooler, souvenirs, etc.

An RV for use on weekends and vacation camping in relatively warm weather is equipped differently from an RV that is meant to be occupied full time or harsher weather conditions. Full-time occupancy requires a different thought process and is covered in Chapter 2.

Three Types of RVs:

The main types of RVs; Towable, Motor Home and Truck Camper a.k.a. Slide-In:

Towable:

A towable hitches directly to the rear of the tow vehicle. Models available can exceed forty feet in length. Tiny RVs can be pulled with a motorcycle. Pop-Ups and Fifth Wheels are included in this group:

Pop Up Trailer

These are lighter weight and can be towed with most midsized SUVs. The lower two to three feet of the walls are solid and usually made of fiberglass. The upper walls are made of vinyl, canvas, or a combination of both. The soft walls, including a door and windows, all collapse providing a low towing profile. Raising the roof creates your living space. A Pop-Up is an inexpensive way to get started in RV camping to see if this vacation style is for you.

Regular Hard Sided Trailer

These have various floorplans that may include not only slide-outs but one or more hinged wall sections which tilt out, a.k.a. expandables, providing additional sleeping area. You can even get a floor plan that includes a **wet bathroom** (combination shower/toilet). Although Pop-Ups and Regular Hard Side Trailers having expandables can be used in cool weather, they are not intended for winter use. A rooftop-mounted air conditioner is an option for the warmer months. There are models with all hard sides that fold up intricately; think origami. The optional Toy Hauler floorplan is described later.

Fifth Wheel Trailer

These RVs are distinctively designed to hitch on to a pickup truck via a special receiver mounted directly over the rear axle. This is more stable than towing other types of trailers. The Fifth Wheel Trailer hitch does not need weight-transfer bars or additional sway control and thus is easier to hitch and unhitch. The hitch occupies a large portion of the pickup bed so it must be removed for other big hauling; this is typically a two-person job.

Motor Home Classes

Motor Homes are differentiated as Class A, Class B and Class C:

Class A These Motor Homes provide the most living space available. Models usually include slide-outs and some have a toy hauler floorplan. Many floor plans provide living areas that can be used with slide-out(s) retracted, but never while driving. Depending on the RV size, there is a choice of diesel or gasoline engines. Larger units with diesel power offer an air-ride suspension system that provide considerable improvement in traveling comfort. Amenities may include a washer/dryer and dishwasher.

Class B Motor Home a.k.a. *camper van*, essentially oversized van with a roof that can be raised, providing to stand-up room inside. They are sufficiently appointed for camping although very compact. Storage is limited and the bathroom is a very small wet bath. A vehicle can be towed behind if you have a correctly sized powertrain. These cramped quarters are not a good choice for full-time living.

Class C Motor Home is characterized by a sleeping area built over the vehicle's cab and built on truck or van chassis. They usually range in length from twenty-seven to thirty-two feet, with a few models up to thirty-five feet. Some floor plans include one or more slide-outs. This RV can be accessorized with a generator, satellite TV system, awnings, auto-leveling system and more. A vehicle can be towed behind if you have a correctly-sized powertrain. Due to limited floor space, a washer/dryer is generally not an option.

Truck Camper a.k.a. Slide-In

The Truck Camper offers a camping solution if you already own a pickup and are ready to move up from tent camping or sleeping outdoors on the ground. They are designed to fit into a pickup truck bed and thus are quite compact. Some models are available with a slide-out that can relieve that claustrophobic feeling.

Truck Campers must carefully be matched to the truck for safety and may require truck suspension modifications, especially if you are considering towing a boat, Jet Ski trailer, or small car.

The dealer will help you match your camper and truck. If you choose to buy from a private party, do your research to ensure you do not overload your truck. Loading and unloading can be accomplished with either attached electric or manually cranked portable jacks. The jacks also can be used as stabilizers while camping.

Features for Selection:

Overall Living Space

You get more living space for your dollar in a Towable than in a Motor Home because it uses the entire frame area for living space, whereas a Motor Home requires area for the driving cab, engine and powertrain. However, please consider that if you must purchase a tow vehicle, the cost advantage may be lost.

Something to Drive When Camped

How will you get to local attractions or the store? Parked at a campsite with a trailer, you can drive the tow vehicle anywhere. But with a Motor Home, you would have to have a vehicle to drive while the Motor Home is left parked. Or, you must put everything away and disconnect all the utilities to drive it locally.

Parking in Tight Places

Towing in general, plus parking, can be challenging. A motor home is easier to park in tight quarters. But if the Motor Home has a vehicle in tow, it is nearly impossible to back up.

Interior Spaces:

Living Area

Stretch out on the couch. Comfortable? Does it pull out or unfold for sleeping? Set it up for sleeping, lie down, and ask yourself if you would rest comfortably there. What are the entertainment options? Is the TV readily viewable from where you would normally sit? Will you use your antenna or RV park cable service? Is it pre-wired for satellite if you prefer?

Slide-Out Room

The addition of a slide-out can add floor space that alleviates that cramped feeling. When choosing a slide-out floorplan consider how much, if any, of the floor space can be used while the slide-outs are fully retracted. For example, is the bathroom, kitchen table or refrigerator accessible to use at a rest stop?

On the downside, slide-outs add weight and cost. Pine cones and other debris can accumulate while parked and cause damage to the top and gaskets during retraction. To avoid having to clear the debris prior to slide-out room retraction, an option is to add roof covers called "slide toppers" that retract like window shades, also adding weight and cost.

SLIDE TOPPER

Bedroom/Sleeping

Smaller RVs offer a full-size bed. The best way to see if this works for you is to lie down on it. It may sound a little silly, but if you and your partner are used to sleeping alone or on a queen/ king, it's best try out the full-size bed. This alone might lead you to consider a larger RV. Many bedroom floorplans do not offer nightstands beside the bed; some offer only one.

Imagine it's time for bed. Where will you put your cell phone? The latest RVs offer bedside USB receptacles for charging your electronics. Are they conveniently located? Take a close look at the closets. How much hanging space is available? RVs never seem to have enough closet space. Somewhere there will be drawers for storage, but it is usually limited. Consider all the clothing you will need and where it will be stored.

Bathroom

How is the bathroom and related storage configuration. The smaller bathrooms have the shower and toilet in the same area called a "wet bath". A bathroom with separate shower and/or tub area is called a "dry bath". Where is the medicine cabinet and is it large enough? Locate the linen storage. Is it sufficient for extra people? If the RV has slide-outs, is there access to a bathroom when they are retracted?

Kitchen/Dining

As the head count goes up in your RV, everything is affected including seating for eating and relaxing. Also consider storage for clothes, personal items, linens and extra food for more people. Sit at the table and imagine it set for two, or perhaps four, or more! Is elbow room at a premium?

How much food storage is available in the cupboards and refrigerator/freezer? Consider storage space for everything you need for food preparation, including staples and seasonings.

Is there storage under the sink for dish soap, trash bags, cleaning and other supplies? Is there enough counter space? What about outlets for your toaster and coffeemaker? So how much counter space is left for food preparation? Perhaps you will forgo food prep and use microwavable meals. Take a close look at the microwave size and power rating. Don't forget the trash can; where does it go?

Refrigerator

What size is the refrigerator/freezer? A typical RV refrigerator is small, and the freezer is tiny. Compare that to the average residential unit of 22.5 cubic feet. How much canned or packaged food and frozen food you want to store is a consideration. RV refrigerator models are powered by 120 volt AC as well as propane gas. There are three-way models available that include a 12 volt DC power option which is not as efficient and will shorten your battery time while "off grid" without added generator.

Larger RVs offer a residential refrigerator that is powered by your RV's battery system via an *inverter* providing 120 volt AC power from a 12 volt DC battery pack. When the vehicle is on the road, the vehicle's charging system keeps the battery pack charged. Larger RVs have larger battery packs to operate the refrigerator while traveling. How long it will keep cold on batteries depends on many factors – outside temperature and humidity, how often the door is opened and to what degree you had set the temperature. Also, remember the battery pack supplies the entire RV while you are off grid so when it's dead, nothing works. Plug in to *shore power* ASAP!

Maintenance/Repair Costs

These are higher overall for a Motor Home because it is usually serviced by an RV dealer. A tow vehicle can be serviced almost anywhere.

Do You Need or Want?

Automatic Leveling System

If you have a gas refrigerator the RV **must** be level when parked. You will also find it quite uncomfortable inside if the RV is-out-of-level. When parked, before you unhitch, you must check for levelness. Use a hand-held bubble level or an app on your cell phone to check the floor front-to-back and side-to-side to see how close to level it is. If adjustments are necessary, drive the RV forward and place leveling blocks behind the wheels and then back the RV onto them. Recheck the levelness and repeat the process. With a small, lightweight RV this isn't a big deal, but with a big heavy rig, leveling can be labor intensive.

After a long day of driving, setting up in extreme weather using blocks will make you say, "There's got to be a better way!" There is! Consider adding an automatic leveling system which will either be hydraulic or electro-mechanical. At the push of a button the RV adjusts to level. This is offered on both a Motor Home and a Towable. When stopping for just one night, the leveling system's legs can be manually lowered just enough to stabilize the RV. If your Towable's site is out of level, it will be necessary to unhitch the tow vehicle before activating the automatic leveling system; otherwise, you could have several thousand pounds of vehicle dangling on the front of your trailer.

Interlocking Leveling Blocks

Generator

Adding a generator, depending on size, can cost thousands of dollars. It is necessary for camping off grid for more than a few days because you would want AC power for air conditioner, microwave oven or residential refrigerator. Otherwise, a generator is like insurance—you don't need it until you need it. Generator fuel options for any RV include propane, gasoline and diesel.

A Motor Home with a built in generator has it connected to the RV's fuel system. Gasoline and diesel models draw fuel from the Motor Home's fuel tank via a tube that sticks up a quarter of the way into the tank. This prevents using up all your driving fuel while running the generator. A propane powered air-cooled generator is much nosier than a comparable diesel water-cooled unit.

The generator noise heard inside the RV can be affected by the quality of its mounting system. If your chosen RV has a generator, run it and sit in the bedroom area. Ask yourself if you could sleep with that unit running. The downside of a generator is that it adds cost and weight. Also, it's been my experience that RV dealers will not give you any significant trade-in value for your generator.

FIFTH WHEEL GENERATOR INSTALLATION

Four Season Rating

To have the flexibility of living in any climate, consider a four-season rated RV. They are marketed as Polar package, Arctic package or Yeti package. While most RV furnaces will keep you warm down to 30°F, the real problem is your water supply freezing. An RV with a four season rating generally offers double-pane windows with a higher wall/ceiling R-rating, which will reduce propane consumption.

The package may also offer heating pads for the holding tanks with the caution that, when using in frigid weather, the tanks must contain a proscribed amount of water to prevent overheating and tank damage. Note: when the heating pads are turned on, all holding tanks must contain water with dump valves closed. After dumping any holding tank, you must put water back in immediately. Refer to your owner's manual for the quantity needed in the tanks for safe heating pad operation.

The dump valves in a four season RV are mounted inside the

heated basement area to prevent them from freezing. Skirting around the exterior a may be required in extremely cold weather—below 0°F when you add windchill factor. For colder climates, some RV parks permit adding external propane tanks/bottles to be placed outside the RV, which you can then connect to your RV propane system. This will minimize the need to refill your onboard propane.

EXTERNAL PROPANE TANK CONNECTION

Toy Hauler

Includes an area in the rear portion of the RV to serve as a mini garage for your toys—motorcycles, dirt bikes and other off-road vehicles. A gasoline tank having a pump can be added for fueling up the toys, eliminating the need to transport fuel in cans. The rear wall of the trailer becomes a fold-down ramp which is spring loaded for ease of use. Some models include fold-down legs to support the ramp so it can be used as a patio deck. Accessories include fold-up or removable railings and screening to convert the deck into a screened-in porch. The interiors are designed with parties in mind; some resemble the inside of a sports bar. If mountain trails or desert dunes are on your itinerary, a toy hauler may deserve consideration.

Extras

If you enjoy sitting outside, consider adding one or more awnings and a floorplan with an optional outside kitchen. Also possible is a separate outside propane grill that slides out of a storage compartment for quick setup.

Buying an RV is a Two-Part Process:

At this point you have your selection preferences well thought out. Armed with the information presented so far in this Chapter, it is time to purchase. Be sure to have your chosen RV looked at by a Certified RV Inspector. It is time to either investigate a private party purchase or go to an RV dealer.

Final Selection and Purchase

At an RV dealer, the sales path you will experience is like the sales path at a car dealership. Whether it is a small mom-and-pop operation or a large RV sales and service center, expect to be greeted by a receptionist who will introduce you to a sales associate who will ask questions. Your answers will help them understand what you are looking for. I expect the sales associate, in your case, will be quite surprised that you know exactly what you want, which will greatly reduce your *lot* walkaround time.

If it's a cold day, dress warmly. RVs on the lot are rarely heated. On a hot day, most of the RVs on the lot will not have the air conditioning running. The exception could be RVs that are "on special" or those they are trying extra hard to sell.

When you have finally chosen your RV, you will be taken into an office to close the deal. Here is where you will be presented with an extended service warranty option. This is a warranty that extends over and above the factory warranty. Before you go to the RV dealer, research online other extended warranty options and prices available. Use this knowledge as part of your negotiation strategy. Remember, the dealer may bury the extended warranty cost into the deal and finance it over possibly twenty years, adding very little to the monthly payment, but you will be paying interest on the extended warranty cost.

Pre-Delivery Walkthrough

This delivery process is the dealer's preparation of the RV. Then your acceptance of the RV.

Unless you started the day early, plan on returning another day to take delivery. Allow several hours for the dealer preparation and delivery process. Pre-delivery services should include filling the propane tanks and putting water in the fresh water tank. The RV will usually come with toilet treatment chemical samples. It is up to the buyer to start up the black water tank. Your sales associate will walk you through operating the various features of the RV, including but not limited to; light switches and control panels, HVAC, kitchen appliances and fold-out sleeping options.

At this point, don't be shy about slowing down the demonstration. Your job is to:

- Open and close everything with a handle or a hinge including windows and their coverings
- Check *all* the lights
- If something moves, move it
- If something turns, turn it
- Look at everything both inside and outside of the RV. There will be small things that need attention. Get them fixed before you leave the lot to save a time-consuming return visit

Insurance

Whatever type of RV you choose; it is imperative that you contact an insurance agent for guidance on selecting an appropriate policy or rider.

2.

Full-Time RVing

Downsizing

It's time to get rid of "stuff". No yard work means no yard tools—mowers, rakes, shovels, etc. When you look at the basement area of a larger RV, consider that a third of it will be taken up by RV accessories. Refer to Chapter 4 about what to keep in your basement. That doesn't leave much room for your things. Think about your current storage needs and reduce that by 95 percent. This includes kitchen, bedrooms, and a garage if you have one. RVs come fully furnished, so all your furniture will have to go.

Dealing with Repairs

Imagine having to pack up your house and transport it to the plumber for repairs! Warranty work typically requires taking your RV to a dealer for repairs. You take your home and park it in the repair center's driveway, then off you go to run errands, visit a restaurant and pass time while repairs are made. This assumes you have a tow/towed vehicle.

When you get back to the dealer, you find they need another day. What do you do? If you have pets, the problem is compounded. Some dealers have a small campground as part of their operation. They will move your RV into their campground where you can stay the night, usually at no charge.

Your Permanent Address

Your "registered domicile" is your permanent address even if you park your RV in a different locale. Your driver's license and other legal documents will contain this address of your registered domicile. It is your base of operations as considered by Federal, State and local jurisdictions. But requirements vary from state to state and are well described at the Escapees RV Club website. Here you will find the details you need along with information on mail forwarding: **https://www.escapees.com/domicile-for-full-time-rvers/**

3

Understanding RV Systems

Electrical

There are two different electrical systems on an RV:

120 Volt AC

This is like the kind in a traditional home. RV park electricity a.k.a. shore power, is supplied via a power pedestal that usually contains one or more 120 volt outlets, a three-prong 30 amp outlet, and may include a four-prong 50 amp outlet.

This powers major appliances; air conditioner(s), microwave oven, clothes washer/dryer, refrigerator, plus some interior lighting and all electrical outlets. These outlets are strategically located throughout the RV living and bedroom areas. GFCIs (ground fault circuit interrupter) will be in kitchen and bathroom areas plus on the exterior. Newer RV models offer 120 volt outlets with USB receptacles for charging cellphones, etc.

The 120 volt system also powers a *converter*/battery charger that keeps the RV battery system charged.

12 Volt DC

This battery system is 12 volts and powers most of the lighting, ceiling vent fans, major appliance circuit boards, furnace and water pump. The tow vehicle electrical system is connected to the RV batteries keeping them charged while driving.

The 12 volt system will have an *inverter* installed if you have a 120 volt residential refrigerator. This *inverter* converts 12 volt DC to 120 volt AC to run the refrigerator when traveling.

A Motor Home will have *two* 12 volt battery systems in addition to the 120 volt system. One is for the vehicle/chassis and one is for the coach. The vehicle chassis battery system is used for engine starting, headlights, brake lights and other vehicle accessories. The coach battery system supplies power to the interior of the coach just as it does in a Towable or Truck Camper.

RV BATTERY BOX

Some RV models offer a 12 volt DC-powered cord winder. At the push of a button, the heavy power cord can be rewound and easily stored. Have a rag handy to clean dirt and debris that can damage and jam the rewind spool.

POWER CORD WINDER

The 12 volt RV batteries differ from automotive batteries; these batteries should **not** be interchanged!

RV batteries are designed to supply a light-to-moderate current load over a long period of time and are usually the lead/acid type. Automotive batteries are designed to supply a high-starting current load over a short period of time.

Propane

To avoid an explosion and fire, before ever moving an RV, **always** turn off the propane tank or bottles at the source. Propane gas is stored as a liquid when under pressure. Propane storage bottles, known as DOT bottles, expire ten years after manufacture. At that time, they must be recertified or replaced. A twin bottle setup has a regulator assembly with a two position valve that automatically transfers the flow over to the full tank when the other tank has emptied.

Motor Homes typically have a permanent propane tank called an ASME tank or may not have a propane system. When fueling the Motor Home with either gas or diesel, ensure the propane is turned **off** at the source.

Most, but not all, propane regulator assemblies have a fuel level gauge. In the absence of a gauge, on a warm day, you can check the propane level by running your hand down the side of the tank. The tank will suddenly feel cold at the level of liquid propane. There may even be a visible frost line. Lastly, on a cold day or when all else fails, simply pick it up. With practice, you can tell by its weight if it is nearly empty.

Propane tanks and bottles should be filled to no more than 80 percent capacity, allowing room for expansion. There is a safety feature on the tanks and bottles called a pop-off valve. This valve will slowly release pressure on an overfilled tank to prevent the tank from bursting, but there is still danger from explosion and fire should the vented propane come into contact with an ignition source. This can include a spark from static electricity, someone's cigarette, and any open flame such as a nearby campfire. In a crash, a broken propane line can ignite causing injury or death and burn the RV to the ground.

Your RV's gas refrigerator will most likely be a two-way. It can be run on propane when parked, requiring a 12 volt DC supply to operate the propane valve system. Alternatively, when shore power is available the refrigerator can be run on 120 volt AC.

If it is a three-way, it can operate solely on 12 volt DC while traveling or parked. However, 12 volt mode creates excessive battery drain. Otherwise it is same as a two-way.

While traveling, always with propane turned off, place some of your reusable freezer packs in the gas refrigerator to keep things cold until you park again.

RVs equipped with propane will also be equipped with an LP gas detector.

Furnace

The RV furnace requires 12 volt DC power both for ignition and blower, and a propane supply for fuel. Install a bug screen on the external exhaust vent.

Furnace Exhaust Vents With Bug Screen

Water Supply and Fresh Water Tank

Fresh potable water for the RV is supplied by a drinking-water-rated hose connected to the RV park water connection. A standard garden hose should **never** be used as it can make the water taste bad and cause heath issues. RV water hoses have thicker walls to prevent kinking and are BPA-free. Camping in below-freezing weather requires a heated hose to prevent a freeze-up.

When using the onboard tank, the system is pressurized by a 12 volt DC-powered pump. The fresh water tank is filled via an externally-capped opening. Some RV models connect the fresh water "fill" to a multifunction switch to make filling the tank easier. Install an external water filter between the park water supply and the RV. It will remove contaminates that can damage components and make the water taste unpleasant.

Water Heater

RV water heaters range in size from four to sixteen gallons. The water is heated by either propane or 120 volt electricity. Most models offer both, which can be used simultaneously to speed up heating time. The power source is selected by a switch on a control panel.

Be sure that the water heater tank is filled before activation! Failure to do so can cause damage, including the possibility of a fire. If your metal tank is not ceramic lined it will also have an anode rod made of zinc; this is sometimes called a sacrificial rod. The rod is designed to corrode before the aluminum, copper or stainless-steel parts corrode. This safety measure protects the tank. The reason for the corrosion is the electrolysis (electric current) generated by dissimilar metals immersed in water. Over time, the rod will self-destruct and should be replaced if large chunks of material are missing. Minor chipping and pitting is normal.

Water Pump

The RV water tank supplies water, via the water pump, when you are not connected to an external water supply. The pump is quite durable and will provide years of trouble-free service. The water pump is powered by 12 volt DC and is controlled by a switch, usually located on the main control panel. When it is first turned on the pump may run for a short while to pressurize the lines, and then shut off. When you draw water from a faucet the pump will start as soon as the pressure falls and may cycle on and off during water delivery. This is normal operation.

Gray Water Tank

The gray water tank is for storage of waste water from the sinks, showers and bathtubs, clothes washer and dish washer. They range from four to fifty gallons or larger. Avoid letting food scraps drain into the gray water tank; they can build up over time, causing clogs and odor. When connected to a sewer, the gray water tank dump valve can normally be left open.

Black Water Tank

The black water tank is for storage of toilet waste. They also range from four to fifty gallons or larger. RV toilets do not have a water tank to hold flush water. They flush with minimal water flow directly from the fresh water system. Unlike the gray water tank, the dump valve(s) must *always* be kept closed to avoid a "pyramid of poo" building up, causing a clog that is expensive to clear.

Most black water tanks are equipped with a flushing system that helps drain the tank. The system has a spray valve, like a lawn sprinkler, which is installed inside the tank. It is connected to a hose fitting on the exterior.

Always use toilet paper designed for RV use. This paper quickly dissolves in water, unlike regular paper which will surely clog your sewer system.

Dump Valve

The RV dump valves are opened and closed via a T-handle. There are separate valves for gray water and black water tanks. To be legal, all sewer outlets must be capped while traveling.

Sewer Hose(s) and Sewer Kit

The sewer hose will drain away all waste water from the RV. This is one of the most important items. Each 10 foot section can contract to fit into its storage area. The hose usually included with an RV is ten feet long, made of cheap material, and is supplied with a single straight fitting for connection to the RV. The intent is for you to place the other hose end, having no fitting, into the park sewer connection. This connection provides no foolproof way to keep the hose from pulling out and spewing sewage everywhere around your site. Ugh! To prevent this, you need not only a sufficient length of hose, but I suggest you add a special elbow fitting on the sewer connection end. This 90 degree elbow has tapered ridges which will allow the fitting to be compatible with park sewer connections of different sizes.

Use caution when selecting hose parts as not all manufacturer connections are interchangeable. Choose sewer fittings with a four-point locking method. Cheaper fittings have a two-point connection that can easily come apart, dumping sewage everywhere! To ensure waste water flows freely to the park drain, use a sewer hose support system. Made of plastic or aluminum, these expand or contract and are tapered to allow good flow. To prevent the hose from drooping between the support sections, add sections of plastic rain gutters. They come in ten-foot lengths from building supply stores. Cut them in half so you can adjust to the required length.

SEWER HOSE SUPPORT

PARK SEWER CONNECTION

The hose itself is stored in a plastic tube that is attached to the bottom front or rear of the RV. It is sometimes stored in a hollow bumper.

Assemble a sewer kit that includes all sewer-related fittings/ accessories. These supplies are readily available from RV supply stores:

- ➤ Plastic container w/tight-fitting lid
- ➤ Hose support
- ➤ Straight and 45 degree clear plastic fittings
- ➤ 90 degree elbow w/tapered ridges
- ➤ Set of weights connected w/plastic strap
- ➤ Reverse flush valve assembly
- ➤ Medical-grade disposable gloves
- ➤ Paper towels

The covered container will prevent odors from spreading into the basement and/or other areas of the RV.

SEWER KIT

Life Safety

The Life Safety items include emergency exit windows, smoke detectors, carbon monoxide detectors, LP gas detectors, fire extinguishers and GFCI outlets.

Emergency Exit Windows – Have a quick-release latch. They may not have screens, and some are designed to break away, falling to the ground. Test them routinely to ensure they open. Use caution when testing, opening only a short way as some have a breakaway one-time-use-only hinge.

Detectors – Test detectors by pressing the test button prior to each trip. Smoke detectors should typically be replaced ten years after the date of manufacture, found on the back of the unit. Should the LP Gas Detector alarm sound, turn off propane supply at the source. The LP gas detector and/or carbon monoxide detector is usually good for five to seven years. You should verify the manufacturer's recommended replacement interval on all your detectors.

Fire Extinguisher – Always are dry chemical type. Check for expiration date and ensure any pressure gauge shows the unit is still ready for use.

GFCI Outlets – Designed to be very highly sensitive to incoming/outgoing current conditions in order to protect people from electric shock. Water is extremely conductive to electricity which is why they are mandated near water sources; kitchen, bathroom and exterior. So, if you touch your potentially defective toaster and then touch the metal sink (which is grounded), the GFCI will "trip". Another situation is standing on wet ground while plugging in your awning lights or electric grill. The GFCI is really *Life Safety*.

4

Your RV's First Outing

Think of your RV as a brand-new furnished apartment that you will stay in for a few days. Your shopping list may seem long but wise choices, along with adequate preparation, will make for a happy journey.

Before You Head Out:

Kitchen

Weight is always a factor in an RV. For dishes and glassware, consider plastic only. When selecting pots and pans, go with lighter materials and leave you old camping cast iron at home. For utensils, consider smaller and lighter items designed with an RV in mind. Be sure to include a can opener. For flatware, again small and light is best; do you really need service for twelve? Remember to stock up on cloth kitchen towels and dishcloths. Many RVs don't have a paper towel holder and what about storage space? Pack the cabinets to minimize movement of items you store. There are many accessories available at RV supply stores to organize things and keep them in place; for example, spring-loaded rods put in cabinets prevent heavy items from forcing the door open, wireframe shelves double shelf space, and a variety of containers or bins.

The small appliances you add are determined by your meal preparation plans. At a minimum consider a toaster/oven, coffee maker and perhaps a small blender. Choose mini appliances, as storage fills up fast.

Bathroom(s)

You will need towels for the bathroom. Stocking RV toilet paper is most important; it is designed to quickly dissolve. Household toilet paper or that recommended for septic tanks will clog your sewer system.

Use small plastic baskets in the bathroom cabinets to organize items so that you won't end up with a jumbled-up maze of supplies. Ensure your bottle and container caps are always tight, as they can come loose when traveling.

Add a small plastic toilet brush/ holder to make that cleaning task easier. Before using the toilet, add one gallon of fresh water along with your choice of treatment. Treatment chemicals come in liquid and solid forms designed to liquefy solids and control odor. Solid forms include tablets and self-dissolving packets.

RV Toilet

Before your trip, start the black water tank by adding a chemical treatment that will liquefy solids and control odors. . Use a weight to keep the sewer hose in place on the park connection, as the force of flow can dislodge it, sending sewage everywhere.

Closets

Closet space is always in short supply! Will you be traveling from one climate to another? When RV shopping, take along a tape measure and note the total length of closet rod available. Comparing this to what you have in your permanent home is laughable. Closets in RVs are not exceptionally tall so storage on the closet floor may not be much of an option other than for shoes. But tall shoes and work boots can catch on the clothes hanging above. Consider adding a clothes rack to hang on a sturdy door.

What to Carry in Basement?

➢ Plastic storage containers to keep things organized
➢ Twenty-foot length of drinking-water-rated hose. It is best to carry a second twenty-foot length should RV park water connection be an excessive distance away
➢ Duct tape
➢ Extra flashlight and hand lantern
➢ Power Surge Protector
➢ Portable automotive compressor, 12 volts with cord and air hose long enough to reach all tires. It can be tough to get your rig near a gas station air hose, and this may also save you from being stranded on the side of the road
➢ Suitably sized jack for flat tire
➢ Lug wrench big enough to get the wheel nuts/bolts loose
➢ Two or more jack stands to reduce floor motion when RV is set up

Jack Stand

➢ Tire covers to reduce weathering

Tire Covers

➤ Rags for cleaning your hands, etc.

➤ Medical-grade disposable gloves to always wear when handling sewer components

➤ Sewer Kit

➤ Extra garden hose for sewer flushing plus hose fitting gaskets

➤ Extra twenty feet of sewer hose; there are times when a single twenty-foot section is not enough to reach the park sewer connection. An option is to install a plastic hose carrier on the undercarriage to hold this extra hose

➤ Assortment of automotive fuses to replace every size in your RV

➤ Tool box that is well equipped yet compact. There's always something that "needs fix'n". Include an RV screwdriver. Even better is a battery-operated drill/driver with a selection of different size bits including square bits for RVs. Add a selection of self-tapping sheet metal screws, a.k.a. drill screws. These have square ends. RVs have hundreds of them and they get loose

➤ "Road alligators" are chunks of tire lying on the road which can damage RVs. I hit one once, and it nearly tore off the plastic fender wheel cover on the street side of my fifth wheel; it was flapping in the breeze and about to fly away at any second. With the help of these tools, I was able to affect a roadside repair in minutes and get back underway. An alternative would have been duct tape—unattractive yet effective

➤ Two large channel lock pliers, or two pipe wrenches, for those times when you cannot get a hose connection to seal properly. Or, when you cannot get it off RV park water connection. Or, when the faucet has no handle. Why? Well, you pull in to a campground late, the office is closed, you call and leave a message, but then a good pair of pliers gets the water on

➢ Stool with a single step and fold-up legs "lightweight" for that time when your site is so out of level on the entrance side that it's a long way up to the first RV step

Setting Up at RV Park:

Parking

RV parks are configured with back-in and pull-through spaces. The pull-throughs are generally reserved for short-term campers. Many overnighters simply pull in, connect to the power, and go to bed without unhooking the tow vehicle. The back-in spaces may require that you disconnect the tow vehicle because of space limitations; they are usually lower in cost than the pull-throughs. When you have been driving all day and it's late, the simplicity of parking in a pull-through may be well worth the cost.

If you have a Towable RV, develop your own unhitch checklist of procedures.

If the RV contains a gas refrigerator, the RV must absolutely be level. All RVs are more comfortable when level. After parking, use a bubble level or a cellphone app and place wheel chocks. Alternatively, if out of level, add leveling blocks under the RV wheels. Plastic interlocking blocks are available to simplify the process. Place jack stands if needed for stability.

Check outside for clearance from trees, tables, or other objects in preparation for extending slide-outs.

Connecting:

- ➤ To connect electric power, first ensure the power pedestal breaker is **off.**
- ➤ Plug the power cord into the RV power connection or unspool.
- ➤ Plug the surge protector into the park power pedestal
- ➤ Plug the power cord in to the surge protector.
- ➤ Turn **on** the breaker(s)
- ➤ To connect the water, ensure each connection has it's gasket then connect the optional water filter. Expect some spitting at the sinks inside as there will be air in the lines
- ➤ Turn on the propane supply
- ➤ Prepare to extend slide-outs. During travel, books and clothes or other objects can fall onto the floor, into the path of slide movement. This can cause extensive damage to the slide and the RV interior. Check that the interior slide path is clear of objects. Note: this happened in my RV, so now I first extend my slide-outs just enough for a look-see and retrieval of any object
- ➤ Turn on the air conditioning cooling or furnace, if needed, so the interior will soon be a comfortable temperature. Alternatively, open the windows
- ➤ At the RV main control panel, turn on water heater. Also, if yours is a residential refrigerator, transfer power from inverter to shore power
- ➤ At the refrigerator, if a gas refrigerator, turn it on. If a three-way refrigerator using 12 volt battery power, switch it to either gas or electric

- *Always* wear medical-grade disposable gloves when connecting the sewer hose.
- Place the Sewer Kit container near your RV sewer connection during setup so everything will be within reach when you need it
- Put on the rubber gloves
- Place the clear straight or clear elbow between the RV sewer connection and the first section of drain hose
- Place the sewer support in line with the RV drain and the park sewer connection. The RV drains work best when the drain hose is placed on a downward slope toward the park drain
- Connect the 90 degree elbow with tapered ridges to the end of the sewer hose and place it in the park sewer connection
- Dispose of the gloves
- Lay the sewer hose in the sewer support
- Place the strapped weights over the elbow at the park sewer connection
- Open gray water tank slide valve(s)
- For cable TV, if available, the connection will be at or near the power pedestal
- Extend awning(s), if equipped

Tearing Down for Travel

Prepare Interior:

➤ Odd as it may seem, first go outside and look around your slide-out(s) area to ensure there will be no obstruction when retracting. Bring in and stow anything you had used outside that belongs inside

➤ Pack away anything loose—dishes, glassware, cookware, utensils, salt and pepper shakers, paper towel holders and small appliances. I place coffee pot and paper towel stand in sink protected by a towel, toaster into oven, basket of misc. into microwave

➤ If you have chairs, strap them down. Stow any foldable counters or desk extensions

➤ Latch, hook and strap ALL doors

➤ Close windows for travel

➤ If you have a slide-out(s) ensure the floor area in front of the slide is clear of objects that would prevent free movement. The slide mechanism is very powerful and will crush or damage any object in its way. The object could, in turn, cause extensive damage to the slide system and the RV interior. Turn off air conditioner(s) or furnace

➤ Turn off water heater

➤ If gas refrigerator, turn it off; if 12 volt refrigerator, leave on during travel; if residential refrigerator, transfer to inverter for power

➤ Retract TV antenna and satellite dish, however equipped

➤ Retract all powered awning(s), if equipped

➤ Turn off lights
➤ Retract slide-out(s)
➤ Exit the RV

Prepare Exterior:

➤ Electric – To avoid power surge damage, always turn **off** the pedestal breaker before disconnecting the surge protector and power cord
➤ Unplug the surge protector from the power pedestal
➤ Unplug the power cord from the surge protector
➤ Coil up or spool up the power cord. When coiling up the cord wipe it clean and avoid dragging the plug end across the ground
➤ Water – Turn **off** the water at park water connection and disconnect the drinking water hose. Then disconnect it from the RV connection and coil it up, draining out the water as you go. When it is coiled, connect the hose ends together, preventing water from leaking out during travel, and secure the coil with two or more bungee cords
➤ Gray Water Tank – Close this dump valve first to avoid any contamination when dumping/flushing black water tank
➤ Black Water Tank – Wear medical-grade disposable gloves! Should your tank(s) not be full enough to dump, consider dumping/flushing anyway to avoid carrying extra weight. This full/empty sensor can also become inaccurate, but you will know it is full when the toilet flushes slowly or not at all

➢ Have a separate garden hose dedicated to flushing the black water tank to avoid contaminating the drinking water hose. Connect it to park water connection and other end to external fitting on reverse flush valve assembly. Open black water dump valve, turn **on** water and flush until the flow is clear

➢ Turn **off** the water at park water connection

➢ Close all dump valves

➢ Disconnect the garden water hose from park water connection. Then disconnect it from the RV connection and coil it up, draining out the water as you go. When it is coiled, connect the hose ends together, to prevent water from leaking out during travel, and secure the coil with two or more bungee cords

➢ Sewer – Place the Sewer Kit container near your connection point during teardown so everything will be within reach when you need it. Disconnect the sewer hose from the RV's straight or elbow fitting. Hold the hose waist high, working it hand-under-hand while walking toward the park sewer connection, ensuring all sewage is draining from the hose. Remove the elbow fitting at the park sewer drain. Take just the hose to its carrier tube or hollow bumper, place inside and secure

➢ Pick up the weight and both hose fittings, place into sewer kit container, secure lid and put in basement.

➢ Dispose of the rubber gloves

➢ Pack up and store away any sewer hose support equipment.

➢ Coil up and store the TV cable connection, if used

➢ Remove and stow wheel covers, if used

> ➤ Stow away the jack stands, if used
> ➤ Store the step stool, if used
> ➤ Turn **off** propane supply completely
> ➤ Start the black water tank by adding a chemical treatment that will liquefy solids and control odors
> ➤ Lock the door
> ➤ Fold up and secure stairs
> ➤ Fold over and secure grab bar
> ➤ Retract any manually operated awning(s)

Walkarounds:

> ➤ Do a walkaround to look for anything on the ground you may have forgotten to put away
> ➤ Look underneath the RV for obstacles or equipment
> ➤ Look at the roof to be certain antenna(s) are retracted
> ➤ If you have a Towable RV, develop your own hitch-up checklist of procedures
> ➤ Remove and stow wheel chocks, if used.

Now you are almost ready to depart. Before driving away do a final walkaround to check of ALL chassis lights.

Maintenance

Tires

Regularly inspecting your tires is critical to preventing tire failure. Improperly inflated tires are the primary cause of failure. Check your tire pressure before each trip and adjust as necessary. Recommended tire pressures can be found on an information plate located on the front street side of the RV. Include a DC powered automotive compressor with your RV. It is operated via any 12 volt battery and is easy to use. But it's never easy to maneuver your RV up to a gas station air pump.

Batteries

At the beginning of each camping season, and every six months, check the 12 volt battery water level and top it off as necessary with distilled water. Also check to ensure all connections are tight and there isn't any corrosion around the terminals. There are commercially available products that can be applied to the terminals and posts to prevent corrosion. This will enhance necessary conductivity.

120 volt Power Cord

Ensure that the large external power cord is undamaged, and the plug pins are straight and free of corrosion. I highly recommend the addition of a surge protector. It protects the RV's delicate electronics from power surges caused by lightning and other power grid surges. It also protects against incorrectly wired power pedestals. Some models will warn you of low or high voltage. They range in cost from $80 to $350 or more depending on size and features.

RV SURGE PROTECTOR

Generator

Requires periodic oil and filter changes, along with cooling system maintenance, if applicable. Run the generator monthly for *use* maintenance.

Fresh Water Tank

Prior to its first use, and before each camping season, sanitize the water tank to kill any accumulated bacteria. The procedure varies slightly with each RV but generally involves filling the tank and plumbing, including the water heater, with water to which bleach has been added (one ounce per eight gallons of water). The system can be drained, after about twelve hours, then flushed with potable water. Consult your RV owner's manual for specific instructions.

Be sure to use an external water filter from an RV supply store. The least expensive are disposable and easily connected in line with the water hose.

Water Heater

Install a bug screen on the exterior air vents on the water heater cover. Insects like to build nests in these openings. They can cause poor or no operation which could cause a fire. Custom-sized screens are available for different water heaters and are easily installed. Do not use window screen material; it can restrict air flow and cause overheating, which can cause fire. At the beginning of the season, fill the water heater from a fresh water source rather than drawing down your onboard supply.

WATER HEATER COVER WITH BUG SCREEN INSTALLED

Water Pump

Inspect the water pump annually for signs of leakage. Some models have a sediment bowl to collect debris; this should be emptied as needed. Ensure all connections are tight to prevent leaks and keep air out of the system.

Dump Valve

RV dump valves are designed for years of trouble-free operation. However, after a period, they will become sluggish and difficult to open. A drain lubricant is available from RV supply stores. Place the lubricant directly into the tank and drive for a few miles to slosh things around. When you begin to drain the tanks, you should see an improvement in valve operation. It may take more than one application for satisfactory results. Beware: RV dealers charge extra to service sewer (yuk) issues.

Furnace

Before each trip, then weekly when traveling, check to ensure the external bug screen is free of insects and debris. Inside the RV, ensure the cold air return and all vents are free of floor debris or rugs etc.

Roof

RV roofs are designed to provide years of trouble-free service. Roofs are made of metal, fiberglass or rubber. It is best to take your RV to the dealer for an annual roof inspection, also for its maintenance. The smallest roof leak can cause wall de-lamination, mold and wood rot. That damage may not be visible for years. When it comes to trade-in time, one of the questions always asked during the appraisal is "Have you had the roof serviced annually?"

If you are confident to safely access your roof, inspect for cracks in the seam sealant and for damage from flying debris. Do-it-yourselfers must ensure the correct sealant because using an incorrect sealant can be worse than no sealant repair at all.

Slide-Out Room

Lack of maintenance on these units could cause failure to extend or retract. If specifically a mechanical failure it could mean hours or days of delay while you wait for an RV field service technician to arrive and make repairs. Slide mechanisms require routine lubrication to ensure free movement. Refer to your owner's manual. Do not lubricate slide rails or gears with automotive wheel bearing grease as it can collect dirt and debris, which can damage the system. A dry lube product in a spray can is available from RV supply stores.

Slide Gaskets

These are rubber gaskets that keep weather and bugs out. Keeping them pliable and add years to their life by regularly spraying them with a special RV gasket treatment available at RV stores.

Troubleshooting

Electrical:

120 volt AC

For a total power failure first check the park power pedestal to ensure power is turned **on**. This is actually a circuit breaker(s). Most problems with the 120 volt system originate at the RV breaker panel. Circuit breakers are designed to prevent fire caused by overloaded circuits or faulty wiring. Beware of over using multiple outlet adapters.

Check the RV breaker panel's main breaker(s) to ensure it is on. Your RV may not have a GFCI breaker. Instead one or more outlets will have integrated GFCI protection, with a "reset" and "test" button.

To troubleshoot lack of power to one or more outlets, look for a breaker that is halfway between on and off. This is the "tripped" position. Turn the breaker **off**, wait a moment, then turn **on** again to restore power. Should that breaker trip again, unplug everything you know to be on that circuit and reset the breaker. If it trips yet again, do not reset it! It is time to seek the services of a qualified RV technician.

If it had not immediately tripped then, one at a time plug in and operate each device. Whenever the breaker trips, you have found the culprit.

12 volt DC

Should the entire RV's DC power be inoperative, go to the battery compartment(s) to locate the DC disconnect switch(es), usually a red knob. It is a simple on/off rotating switch that disconnects all battery power. Turning this to the **on** position should bring the RV to life. Although this battery switch is manually operated, it could have inadvertently been left in the *off* position during maintenance.

The battery system is protected by numerous self-resetting DC breakers located in the battery compartment. Failure of one of these breakers will render that entire DC subsystem inoperable. These breakers sometimes begin to trip/reset intermittently when either the slide system or leveling system is operated. If replacing the affected breaker does not clear the problem, it is time for service by a qualified RV technician. Remember, circuit breakers and fuses are Life Safety devices designed to prevent fires

Problems with inoperative lights or appliances can usually be corrected by replacing the appropriate automotive-type fuse, located in the DC fuse panel. Make sure you replace the blown fuse with one of the correct value. The fuse location and value are listed on a placard inside the fuse panel door. Do not install a fuse with a higher value than specified, as this could cause a fire. If the fuse blows again, seek the help of a qualified RV technician.

The 12 volt chassis system is powered by the tow vehicle via a cable for trailer lights. It operates electric brakes, tail lights, turn signals and any marker lights. A Motor Home has it integrated within the overall electrical system. Fixing a single light could be as simple as replacing the pluggable bulb or LED. If that does not work, you should check the light fixture for moisture intrusion, corrosion (a white chalky powder and/or green around the terminal cable connections) or a loose connection. Correct each problem with its specific remedy.

Should none of the RV exterior chassis lights operate, check to make sure there is a firm connection into the tow vehicle. If still not working, check that the recessed plug prongs (male) in the covered plug of the tow vehicle are free from debris, or only have light corrosion. Similarly examine the trailer cable receptacle (female) end. Wipe away all debris with a rag or swab. Light corrosion can be removed using white vinegar with a swab. Note: if there is heavy corrosion or extensive damage, have it repaired by a qualified RV technician.

Refrigerator

Residential refrigerators operate strictly on 120 volt AC. If not working, check the refrigerator circuit breaker in the RV breaker panel.

If the gas refrigerator will not get cold or has not stayed cold, check the DC fuse panel to see if it is blown. Next check the power source setting on the refrigerator. If set to propane, ensure there is propane in the tank and the shutoff valve is turned **on**. If the source is switched to electric, is the RV plugged in to shore power? Next check that the refrigerator circuit breaker in the RV breaker panel is not tripped.

Whenever food in the refrigerator compartment freezes, be sure the temperature adjuster is still attached to the cooling fins inside; it is not unusual for it to be jarred loose during a rough ride. Or, perhaps your refrigerator has external temperature controls on or between the doors, which should never be set below 33° F or above 40°F. Verify internal temperatures with an inexpensive appliance thermometer.

Water Heater

Your RV water heater will most likely be two-way. It can be run on propane, requiring a 12 volt DC supply to operate the propane valve system. Alternatively, when shore power is available, the water heater can be run on 120 volt AC. It is possible to turn on both sources, temporarily, to rapidly heat the water.

If there is no hot water, is the water heater turned **on**? At the main control panel, check if the propane switch is turned on, ensure there is propane in the tank and the shutoff valve is turned on. If the 120 volt switch is turned on, are you plugged into shore power? Check that the water heater circuit breaker in the main power panel is not tripped.

If the water supply is not very hot, make sure that both hot and cold faucets are fully shut off at the external shower station. Should these valves be left open, all the hot water will be diluted with cold water. Make it a habit to completely turn off these faucets after each use.

Furnace

RV furnaces run on propane. If the furnace fails to start, check for a blown fuse in the 12 volt fuse panel. If the blower starts but there is no heat, make sure there is propane in the tank and the shutoff valve is turned on. If there is still no heat, seek the help of a qualified RV technician.

Slide-Out

Common problems can include failure to extend or retract, pausing or stopping when extending or retracting or noise when operating. A complete failure of a slide is most likely an electrical problem and is best repaired by a qualified RV technician. In an emergency, most slide systems can be moved in or out using a hand crank or battery-operated drill. Refer to your owner's manual.

Plumbing

Interior water leaks may appear from time to time. The RV is subject to vibration while moving which can loosen drain line and water connections. These can usually be fixed by hand tightening the fitting. If pliers are needed, use minimal force as the fittings are made of plastic so can easily be broken.

Drains

Clogging of sink or shower drains can often be remedied easily by emptying the **gray water tank**. This may sound overly simple, but if you forget to open the gray water tank drain valve after setup in the park, you're running on borrowed time. The full/empty sensor can become inaccurate, but you will know it is full when the drains aren't doing their job. RV sinks can become clogged just like a home sink. The difference here is that you cannot use harsh unclogging chemicals because they can damage gaskets and seals.

Use an appropriately sized plunger or drain snake

> ➤ Pour a half cup of baking soda into the drain, then slowly add a cup and a half of white vinegar
> ➤ Let this sit for one hour then pour in a gallon of hot water

Finally, you may have to take the drain apart to clear it.

Always use medical-grade disposable gloves when working with the sewer system.

A toilet/**black water tank** clog can sometimes be cleared by operating the flush system, if equipped. Although it happens rarely, when black water drain valve is opened, it drains for a short time and then stops.

Extreme caution must be taken when using the flush system on a clog, as the tank can overfill flooding the interior of the RV with sewage.

While you are outside operating the flush system, have someone inside depress and hold down the toilet flush pedal while looking down into the tank. Should water be observed rising, immediately call outside "Turn off the water!" to avoid overflow.

If unsuccessful, use external reverse flush valve assembly with a fitting which allows a garden hose to be attached. This assembly is connected between the main drain hose and the RV sewer connection.

Reverse Flush Valve Assembly Operation:

➤ Close black water drain valve
➤ Detach main drain hose from RV drain
➤ Attach assembly to RV drain
➤ Connect main drain hose to external slide valve assembly
➤ Connect a garden hose to the fitting making sure that you use the included "back check" valve to prevent fresh-water system contamination. Do not use the same hose that you use for your fresh water connection
➤ Close slide valve
➤ Open black water drain valve
➤ Turn water **on** at the park water connection
➤ Also turn water **on** at reverse flush valve assembly
➤ Observe water level through the clear plastic piece as the pipe fills. Listen for a loud gurgle. This indicates that the clog has been pushed back from the tank opening
➤ Turn water **off** at external slide valve assembly
➤ Open slide valve on the assembly, and—whoosh—the tank empties
➤ Visibly check tank by looking into it through the toilet to ensure you have room for flush water. Do not run fresh water more than one minute or you risk flooding the RV with sewage
➤ If a second attempt is needed, have an observer inside the RV watching the toilet's water level rising as before.

EXTERNAL REVERSE FLUSH ASSEMBLY

Water Pump

If the water pump fails to operate when a faucet is opened, first turn on any DC light in the RV to ensure you have adequate battery power. Then check for a blown fuse in the 12 volt fuse panel. Finally, check the pump wiring for loose connections.

If the pump runs continuously, check to ensure all faucets inside and out are closed, and inspect for leaks. Is the fresh water tank empty?

Other failure points can be the pump itself or a multi-position water control switch used to direct the flow which is supplied from either city water or fresh water tank. Both the pump and the multi-position valve can easily be replaced by the do-it-yourselfer.

In Closing

RV camping is an excellent way to leisurely enjoy your vacation travels. You simply pack once, and you get to sleep in your own bed. You can stop along the highway at a rest area to make lunch or take a nap. Many RV parks are located right on a beach while others are considered destination resorts with attractions and entertainment for all ages. I have enjoyed RVing so much that the writing of this Handbook celebrates completion of four years as a full timer RVer!